THE FOUNDATIONS OF WISDOM

VOLUME 3

PHILOSOPHY OF MAN STUDY GUIDE

THE FOUNDATIONS OF WISDOM

VOLUME 3

PHILOSOPHY OF MAN STUDY GUIDE

FR. SEBASTIAN WALSHE, O. PRAEM.

TAN Books

Gastonia, North Carolina

Cover design by Andrew Schmalen

Cover image: The Creation of Adam by Michelangelo, circa 1511, fresco painting / WikimediaCommons, public domain.

ISBN: 978-1-5051-2643-3

Published in the United States by
TAN Books
PO Box 269
Gastonia, NC 28053
www.TANBooks.com

Printed in India

CONTENTS

Introduction

This is a study guide to accompany volume 3, Philosophy of Man, of *The Foundations of Wisdom: An Introduction to the Perennial Philosophy*. In this study guide I will explain the overall structure of volume 3 and how best to read the text of volume 3. I will also include essential, chapter-by-chapter questions you should be asking and answering as you read through the text. The answers to these questions are not all found verbatim in the text itself (though some are). The purpose of these questions is not only to help the student read the text carefully, but also to think about things implied by or related to the teaching in the text. For some of the questions in which the answer is not found explicitly in the text, you may be able to provide only a provisional or probable answer. That is OK. The purpose of those questions is to get the student to think more deeply about the realities indicated in the text.

Logic and Natural Philosophy as Prerequisites to the Study of the Soul

Whenever we try to investigate some subject, we ask a series of questions about it. Some questions cannot be answered unless we know the answers to prior questions. For example, the question "Can virtue be taught?" cannot be answered well without answering the questions "What is virtue?" and "What is teaching?" So it is with the study of the soul. Certain questions about the soul, such as, "What is a soul?" and "Is it certain that the human soul can exist after death?" cannot be answered well without having answered prior questions, such as "How is a good definition constructed?" and "How can we determine if the conclusion to an argument is necessarily true?" Therefore, before embarking upon the study of the soul, it is necessary for the student to acquire the prior sciences of logic (volume 1) and natural philosophy (volume 2). Logic is necessary as a prerequisite for all the speculative sciences, since all of these use definitions, statements and demonstrations. Natural philosophy is a prerequisite to the study of the soul because life is found first in natural things, like trees and dogs and men. Unless we know something about natural things generally, we will not be able to understand particular kinds of natural things well, including those with souls. So if you have not yet studied logic and natural philosophy, you should lay this book aside and study those subjects well before taking up this book again. One way to do this is to start at the beginning of this series, since the previous two volumes in this series consider logic and natural philosophy.

The Need for a Teacher

In the study guides for logic and natural philosophy, I touched upon the need for a teacher in philosophy, or in any difficult matter. The study of the soul is no exception. As Aristotle once wrote about the soul, "To determine anything reliable about it is among the things which are most difficult."[1] Since the study of the soul is among things difficult to learn, requiring much experience, it cannot be learned well simply

[1] Aristotle, *De Anima*, Book I, 402a10.

from a book. There are so many questions which the study of the soul raises that no book could adequately consider all of them without becoming too large. No book can answer questions the way a teacher can, and so, no book, by itself, is sufficient as a guide for the life of the mind. Therefore, once again, I strongly recommend that, in addition to reading this book on the study of the soul (together with this study guide), try to find someone who already knows this subject matter well who can fulfill the role of a teacher.

The Overall Plan of the Study of the Soul

This book is divided into three parts. In the first part (Introduction and chapter 1) I cover some preliminaries to the study of the soul. In the second part (chapters 2–11), I consider the soul itself. In the third part (chapter 12), I consider and refute subjectivism, which is an erroneous account of knowledge.

In the consideration of the soul itself, I first consider the definition of soul (chapter 2), then I consider the specific kinds of soul (for example, the vegetative soul, the sentient soul, and the rational soul) and the properties which belong to each of them (chapters 3–11).

Using Supplementary Texts

Some chapters refer the student to supplementary texts in the footnotes. These texts are, for the most part, original texts of great thinkers. Depending upon the abilities of the teacher and students, as well as upon the time you have to complete the course, these supplementary texts can be very helpful to examine a subject in greater detail. If the teacher is knowledgeable and familiar with these supplementary texts, and the students are more advanced, these texts will be very helpful for increasing the student's knowledge of the study of the soul. However, the course can be completed without reading the supplementary texts. They are options for those who desire to use them.

How Much Reading and Study Time Should Be Devoted to Each Part?

The time needed to cover the materials in this book is the sum of the time it takes to read the book and cover the material in class. The amount of time it should take a student to read the book carefully is approximately 20 hours. The amount of class time to cover the contents of this book should total to somewhere between 45 and 65 hours. So a student should expect that the total amount of time necessary to cover the entire contents of the study of the soul book with this accompanying study guide will be between 65 and 85 hours.

As a ballpark figure, chapters 1–4 should take approximately 15–20 hours to read and discuss; chapters 5–11 should take approximately 40–50 hours to read and discuss; and chapter 12 should take approximately, 10–15 hours to read and discuss.

These are simply estimates based upon my experience teaching this material. There may be reasons or circumstances why a particular student might use significantly more time than what is recommended here, but it would be unusual that a student would need significantly less time than the 65 hours recommended here.

List of Definitions for the Study of the Soul

Soul (nominal) (ch. 1): The first principle of life in a living thing; or Whatever is ultimately responsible for the difference between living and non-living things.

Soul (essential) (ch. 2): The substantial form of a natural, living body.

Nutrition (ch. 5): The assimilation of food into the substance of a living body.

Growth (ch. 5): The assimilation of food into the quantity of a living body.

Reproduction (ch. 5): The assimilation of food into the seed of a living body; or Bringing into existence, from seed, another living substance of the same kind.

Vegetative power (ch. 5): A power of the soul by which a living being produces another living being of the same kind as itself.

Sensation (nominal) (ch. 6): Whatever seeing, hearing, smelling, tasting and feeling all have in common.

Sensation (essential) (ch. 6): The reception of the forms of the affective qualities of another thing, as other; or The reception of the forms of the affective qualities of another thing in an immaterial way.

Sense Power(ch. 6): The ability to receive the forms of affective qualities of another thing, as other.

Knowledge (ch. 12): The possession of the form of another thing, as other.

Understanding (ch. 6): The ability to possess the "what it is" of things sensed or imagined, as other.

Intellectual Power (ch. 9): The ability to know order, as such.

Rational Power (ch. 9) The ability to come to know one truth from another truth.

Introduction and Chapter 1

What to Look for in the Introduction and Chapter 1

Look for the reasons why you should be very motivated to study the soul. Also, try to understand why we should begin the study of the soul with a definition of soul based upon our experience of our own living activities. Finally, try to see how the study of the soul is related to other kinds of knowledge.

Summary and Explanation of the Introduction and Chapter 1

The introduction gives reasons why the student should diligently study the soul, namely, because of the certitude of knowledge we can have (since we are certain of our own living activities); because of the nobility of the soul as a subject of knowledge; and because of the utility of knowledge about the soul.

Chapter 1 explains where we should begin the study of the soul. We should not begin with customary ideas about the soul, not only because many of them are unfounded, but also because many customary ideas about the soul are mutually exclusive. So, the best place to begin is to recognize the connection between life and the soul, and with this in mind to formulate a nominal definition of the soul. After responding to the possible misunderstandings that such a definition may cause, the chapter goes on to identify the place of the study of the soul within the whole body of knowledge.

Questions about the Introduction and Chapter 1

How can it be true that knowledge of the soul is certain when there is so much disagreement about the soul, even about whether souls exist?

Why is the soul noble?

Granted that certain knowledge is good and that knowledge about noble things is good, what makes a knowledge better: the certitude of the knowledge, or the nobility of the thing known?

What is knowledge of the soul useful for?

How does a nominal definition differ from a definition by properties or an essential definition?

Is the nominal definition proposed in the text a good definition, especially since it would mean that all living things, even plants, have a soul?

Why is the study of the soul included as a part of natural philosophy? What does this imply about the order in which we should study these two sciences?

Chapter 2

What to Look for in Chapter 2

Notice how our previous study of logic and natural philosophy enters into the construction of an essential definition of the soul. Pay attention to how common experiences of life and living things are the key contacts with reality which allow us to move from a merely nominal definition to a definition of a really existing thing.

Summary and Explanation of Chapter 2

Chapter 2 begins by using the tools of logic (such as the ten Categories) and the distinctions made in natural philosophy (such as the distinction between matter and form) to construct a definition of the soul. Next, the definition is confirmed by testing it against experience and against the four marks of a good definition. Finally, some corollaries about the soul are derived from the essential definition of the soul.

Questions about Chapter 2

How do we know that there is such a thing as a soul?

Why can't the soul be an accident?

Why can't the soul be a body or a complete substance?

What common experiences are foundational for the essential definition of the soul?

Why is the statement that "soul and body are united" self-evident and *per se*?

Why can't we say that the relationship of the body and soul is like that of a driver and a car? What makes that relationship uniquely different?

Chapters 3 and 4

What to Look for in Chapters 3 and 4

Try to understand why it is important to investigate the powers of the soul in order to know the different kinds of soul more perfectly. Clearly distinguish the different kinds of parts and wholes by understanding their definitions. Finally, compare the method by which we come to understand the powers of the soul with your experience of coming to know any ability.

Summary and Explanation of Chapters 3 and 4

Chapter 3 begins by explaining why we might say that the soul has parts. Next, it considers the chief meanings of whole and part. Finally, it concludes that the soul has parts in the sense of powers, or potential parts. Chapter 4 shows from experience the order in which we come to know the powers of the soul beginning from the better known objects of these powers.

Questions about Chapters 3 and 4

Since we already have a definition of soul, why bother investigating the powers of the soul?

What experiences would make someone think that the soul has parts?

What are the definitions of integral whole, universal whole, and potential whole?

What kind of whole is the soul? How does understanding the different types of wholes help us understand how the soul functions?

How do we know that the soul is a potential whole?

Why can't we know the powers of the soul before the activities of the soul? Why can't we know the activities of the soul before their objects?

Chapter 5

What to Look for in Chapter 5

Try to understand the key reasons why plants should be distinguished from machines. Pay careful attention to the exact meaning of the term "object" when it is said that food is the object of the vegetative power.

Summary and Explanation of Chapter 5

Chapter 5 begins a detailed investigation of the various powers of the soul which concludes in chapter 11. First, the vegetative power is considered (in chapter 5), next the sensitive power (in chapters 6–8), then the rational power (in chapters 9–10). Finally, the desiring powers belonging to the sense and rational powers are considered (in chapter 11).

The consideration of the vegetative power begins by explaining why we should begin an investigation of the powers of the soul with the vegetative power, and then answering the question whether plants are truly alive. This question must be answered in order to justify the claim that plants have a soul as we have defined it. After this, the object and activities of the vegetative power are considered in order to formulate a definition of the vegetative power. Finally, a few difficult or boundary cases are taken up, such as viruses and DNA, in order to clarify what is meant by calling something a living being.

Questions about Chapter 5

Why should we study the vegetative power before the sense power when the sense power seems better known to us?

Why can't all the differences between plants and non-living things be explained by purely mechanistic causes?

What role does our own experience of performing activities, like nutrition and reproduction, play in coming to recognize plants as alive?

When it is said that food is the object of the vegetative power, what does "object" mean? Can food be defined apart from the vegetative power? Is food the object of an active or passive power?

Why is reproductive activity sufficient for defining the vegetative power?

Are viruses or DNA alive, simply speaking?

Chapter 6

What to Look for in Chapter 6

Trace the steps involved in moving from a nominal definition of sensation to an essential definition of sensation. Try to see why sensation is not just a physical change like alteration, and why sensation requires some kind of immateriality. Form a clear understanding of why sensation is a kind of mean between understanding and alteration. Also, try to see how it is possible for sensation to put us in contact with real things outside of us.

Summary and Explanation of Chapter 6

The first part of chapter 6 is dedicated to arriving at an essential definition of sensation and of the sense power. This begins from a nominal definition and ultimately concludes with an essential definition. The key step in this movement is distinguishing sensation from alteration. Once sensation has been defined, the chapter goes on to consider the various kinds of objects of sensation.

Questions about Chapter 6

How do we arrive at a nominal definition of sensation?

What fundamental and evident experiences of living activities allow us to come to the essential definition of sensation from the nominal definition?

Why can't sensation just be a form of alteration?

Why does sensation require immateriality?

Why does sensation have to be of another thing? What about the fact that we can see our own eyes in a mirror, for example?

Given the fact that many people disagree about what they are sensing, how can we be certain that our senses put us in contact with real things?

Why might sensation be confused with understanding? How is sensation a mean between alteration and understanding?

Since the common objects of sensation are obviously sensed through the proper objects, why aren't they sensed *per accidens*?

Chapter 7

What to Look for in Chapter 7

Try to understand why the external senses are essentially different kinds of sensation. Also try to understand the order among them. In particular, try to understand in what way the sense of touch is one sense and in what way it is many senses.

Summary and Explanation of Chapter 7

Chapter 7 takes up the external senses one-by-one and explains the objects and activities of these senses in order to arrive at definitions of each of the powers of these external senses. Finally, the chapter concludes with an explanation of the order among the external senses.

Questions about Chapter 7

Given the definition of sensation, and granted that a species-making difference signifies how a thing is what it is, can you show why different degrees of immateriality result in essentially different kinds of sensation?

Why is it that if a tree falls in a forest with no one to hear it, it does not make a sound in the strict sense of the term "sound?" (As a discussion question, can you work out how this is not simply relativism disguised?)

Why would someone say that touch is many senses? Why would someone say that it is only one sense?

Why are the external senses ordered in the way they are?

Why do we have multiple external senses instead of just one?

Why does each sense require a medium?

What evidence do we have to show that the objects of the external senses are real things outside of us?

Why are sight and hearing more refined and thus defined and more noble than touch and taste?

Chapter 8

What to Look for in Chapter 8

Try to determine why it is necessary to assert that we have internal senses in addition to external senses. Try to understand why there are only four internal senses, and how they are distinguished from each other. Finally, pay attention to the experiences which force us to conclude that there are four internal senses.

Summary and Explanation of Chapter 8

Chapter 8 begins with some initial observations about experiences which cannot be explained in terms of the external senses alone, and then goes on to distinguish four internal senses corresponding to these experiences. Next, this chapter takes up each internal sense individually, explaining and defining them. Finally, the chapter concludes with a brief consideration of the way in which some internal senses are tied to morality.

Questions about Chapter 8

What experiences force us to conclude that in addition to our external sense, we must also have internal senses?

More specifically, what experiences are the foundation for distinguishing each of the four internal senses?

Do animals have these internal senses? If so, how do they operate differently in men than in animals?

What is the object of each of the internal senses?

What is the definition of each internal sense?

How do we know that there are only four internal senses?

How do the internal senses operate in relation to each other?

How do they operate in relation to reason?

Chapter 9

What to Look for in Chapter 9

Try to understand which experiences require that the rational power is really distinct from the sense powers. Carefully evaluate the arguments for the immateriality and immortality of the human soul to see if they can be reduced back to necessary and self-evident statements.

Summary and Explanation of Chapter 9

The first part of chapter 9 is dedicated to distinguishing the rational power of the human soul from the sense powers, and to arriving at a definition of the rational power based upon the objects of reason. The second part is dedicated to proving that the rational soul can exist apart from the body and that it is immaterial. Finally, additional questions are considered as a consequence of this doctrine (for example, the possibility of reincarnation).

Questions about Chapter 9

What ordinary experiences lead us to distinguish sensation from reason?

What are some objects of reason which are in no way an object of the external or internal senses?

What definition of reason implicitly contains all of the objects proper to reason?

Granted that all knowledge, even sense knowledge, implies some kind of immateriality, how is the immateriality required for rational knowledge different from the immateriality required by sense knowledge?

What is the fundamental reason why the power of reason cannot be the act of a bodily organ, nor can it act through a bodily organ?

What are some objections to the position that the rational power does not have a bodily organ? How can they be resolved?

How can a form exist without its proper matter?

Is immortality the same as immateriality? If not, what is the reason for their connection?

If the same individual soul can exist after death, why isn't reincarnation possible?

Chapter 10

What to Look for in Chapter 10

Try to understand why it is necessary to posit an active and passive power in the intellect. Also try to understand the process of abstraction, and why it is necessary. Finally, try to understand why an agent intellect would not cause us to actually know everything knowable by the human mind.

Summary and Explanation of Chapter 10

The chapter begins by pointing to an experience which needs to be explained: the movement from potency to act in our intellectual knowledge. Next, an argument is made to show that to explain this movement, both active and potential intellectual powers must be at work in the intellect. Finally, abstraction is explained by way of an analogy to sensible light.

Questions about Chapter 10

Why does every motion require a mover which is active as well as a thing moved which is passive? How does this show that there must be an active and passive principle in the human intellect?

What is abstraction, and how is it possible for material things to affect an immaterial power like the intellect?

What is the importance of saying that the agent intellect possesses all forms virtually?

Why is it true to say that there is nothing in the intellect which has not first passed through the senses?

Chapter 11

What to Look for in Chapter 11

Try to understand why it is necessary to posit an appetitive, or desiring, power in the soul in addition to the knowing powers already discussed. Attend to the reasons why every knowing power implies an appetitive power. Finally, try to understand the exact relationship between knowing and desiring.

Summary and Explanation of Chapter 11

Chapter 11 begins with a brief account of the experiences which lead us to deduce the existence of appetitive powers in the soul. Next, the sense appetite is considered, followed by a consideration of the rational appetite. Finally, there is a brief consideration of the priority of knowledge to appetite.

Questions about Chapter 11

What living experiences can only be explained by some kind of appetitive power distinct from knowing powers?

Why must every knowing power have a corresponding appetitive power?

What is the object of the sense appetite as distinguished from the object of the rational appetite?

Why must the rational appetite rule over the sense appetite?

How are the concupiscible and irascible appetites distinguished? Is this an essential distinction, or merely an accidental distinction in the appetite?

Since the will can move the intellect, and in general an appetitive power can move a knowing power to act, why is it true to say that the rational and sense knowing powers are prior to the rational and sense appetites?

Chapter 12

What to Look for in Chapter 12

This chapter is especially focused upon refuting "soft subjectivism," that is, the position that we know our own thoughts and sense impressions better than we know the things that produce them. If we can refute soft subjectivism, all the other doctrines such as moral and intellectual relativism are destroyed. Therefore, pay closest attention to the arguments for subjectivism and the refutation of those arguments. Attend especially to how the subjectivists are using an incomplete and faulty definition of knowledge, and how human experience demands that knowledge be defined differently than the definition used by the subjectivists.

Summary and Explanation of Chapter 12

Chapter 12 begins with an explanation of five related doctrines which are common theories of knowledge in modern philosophy. These five doctrines are subjectivism ("hard" and "soft"), intellectual relativism, moral relativism, and skepticism. After showing the dependence of all of these doctrines upon soft subjectivism, the chapter goes on briefly to refute the most radical positions (skepticism and moral relativism). The remainder of the chapter is devoted to refuting soft subjectivism.

The refutation of subjectivism begins with some arguments in favor of subjectivism, followed by a critique of these arguments. Next, positive arguments against subjectivism are presented. Finally, the chapter concludes by identifying the key error of subjectivism, namely, a faulty definition of knowledge.

Questions about Chapter 12

How has intellectual custom played a role in strengthening the arguments for subjectivism, relativism, and skepticism?

How are relativism and skepticism dependent upon subjectivism?

What is soft subjectivism versus hard subjectivism? Why does soft subjectivism ultimately lead to hard subjectivism?

Why is it easier to refute skepticism and relativism than it is to refute subjectivism?

What aspects of human experience, especially sensation, support some of the claims of subjectivism?

How can those same experiences be explained by someone who denies subjectivism?

What kinds of errors are found in the arguments for subjectivism?

How do logic and the study of the soul help to identify and refute these errors?

Show how the definition of knowledge presupposed by the subjectivists ignores fundamental aspects of our experience of knowledge.

More often than not, what is moral relativism a mask for?

If things cannot be known in themselves, and there is no objective standard of right or wrong, what are the practical consequences for the way in which powerful people will treat weak people?

Why can't our own knowing power be the first object of our knowledge? Why can't our activity of knowing be the first object of our knowledge?

General Questions for the Study of the Soul

How are the sciences of logic and natural philosophy presupposed to the study of the soul? Give concrete examples.

How is the natural road (the road from the senses into reason) at work throughout the study of the soul?

Explain each of the powers of the human soul both in themselves and in relation to one another. How are these powers brought together into a formal unity which is directed to a single end?

How has the study of the soul refined the definition of man, and made explicit certain accidents proper to man?

How does the study of the soul point to the need for a branch of philosophy other than logic and natural philosophy?